The Soul Mate Collection

The Soul Mate Collection

SMC

Donald C. Langston

iUniverse, Inc.

New York Lincoln Shanghai

The Soul Mate Collection

iUniverse books may be ordered through booksellers or by contacting:

iUniverse
2021 Pine Lake Road, Suite 100
Lincoln, NE 68512
www.iuniverse.com
1-800-Authors (1-800-288-4677)

ISBN-13: 978-0-595-35865-6 (pbk)
ISBN-13: 978-0-595-80322-4 (ebk)
ISBN-10: 0-595-35865-9 (pbk)
ISBN-10: 0-595-80322-9 (ebk)

Printed in the United States of America

Contents

Introduction

The Soul Mate Collection is expression of the intimate union between a man and woman who are so intricately woven together in heart and thought, they can only be called soul mates. The collection consists of a series of brief poems that seek to capture the coming together, the love shared, the maturing of the relationship, the heartache endured to grow closer, and the continuous efforts to keep the love everlasting.

Relationships are not easy, but when two can come together in love, openness, honesty, trust, communication, commitment, and agreement, there is no stronger union or bond, nor any greater satisfaction under Heaven.

The poems, written over a 10 year period, are my interpretation of the splendor of relationship in all its unique stages. I've had the privilege of living in various parts of the U.S., such as Texas, California, Florida, Louisiana and Oklahoma as well as living overseas in Panama, Japan, and Germany, with visits to Hawaii, Italy, Egypt and the Netherlands. The simplicity and complexity of love and relationship experiences are universal and everyone can identify with the beauty, heartache, heartbreak, twists, turns, highs and lows of making it work.

So, sit back, relax and enjoy this reminiscent journey for some and hopeful expectation for others of the thrills of the Soul Mate relationship.

dcl

SECTION I
When We Met

Call it a chance meeting, a planned evening or a destined encounter, there is a lasting uniqueness about the first time you meet your soul mate. The smallest details about the event become very significant and all important. The ingredients for this splendid recipe can be the time of day, the fragrance in the air, the song that played, the music heard in the background, a crowded place, or the crazy sequence of events that allow you to meet that unforgettable person. All these things bring about an inseparable mix and delightful blend that bonds and holds two hearts together. To explain what happened is an attempt to explain the unexplainable. The very best you can do is welcome, embrace and respond to that uncontrollable uniting with that special someone on that special day.

A WALK WITH YOU

Just a short walk, but so much meaning it did hold
Inquiring all about you, to hear the things untold
Wanting to draw close, listening to every word you speak
Amazed by your beauty, so rare and so unique
Hearing in your voice the deep treasures in your heart
Wanting this to always last, a never ending start
What began as a stroll, just me wanting to walk with you
Will forever be the moment of a dream coming true

AFTERTHOUGHT

I had the rare opportunity to meet my soul mate
Exquisite were the moments, but still so much I didn't relate
So the rest I say to you in an afterthought

Everything about you speaks to me and I understand
The voice of your being talks to me of mysterious things
Questioning and answering the deepest wonderings of my mind
Exploring your untouched regions while ignoring the passage of time

Where are you from, where have you been and where are you going?
The winding path you took that has brought you here
With treasures deposited in your heart that I want to hold near

There's no need to explain your every action
Some things are just the uniqueness of you
Yet there's more to show, still unfathomable things that I want to
    know

Your idiosyncrasies are not a bother
Found cute are your silly ways
That certain word you misuse or the punch line to the joke you abuse

In so many ways we perfectly connect
Seamlessly woven together, no line to detect
I had the rare opportunity to meet my soul mate
Exquisite were the moments, but still so much I want to relate

ANGEL

I beheld an angel enveloped by a radiant light
The splendor of her ways were a heavenly sight
Noble and regal, poised with charm and grace
Beautiful princess with such a lovely face

Such captivating eyes that were wondrous to behold
Showing me mysteries that would soon unfold
The words of her voice took me to another place
Speaking of precious things that time can never erase

I saw the depth of her love and her willingness to give
Now I understand life and what it means to truly live
The places she touched healed scars and wounds
Promising painful memories would also disappear soon

When I'm with her time stops and remains still
Exploring a fantasy that has suddenly become real
Knowing an intimacy that takes me to places beyond
Sharing a bond of closeness that make two seem as one

I beheld an angel enveloped by a radiant light
The splendor of her ways are such a heavenly delight

AT FIRST SIGHT

Some believe assuredly in love at first sight
Until today I wasn't sure they were absolutely right

Call it a change of mind or a change of heart
My first glimpse of you caused love to start

Not an overwhelming emotion or a loss of control
Rather I heard unspoken words that captivated my soul

A loss of concentration with your every pose
Like viewing daybreak as a lovely sun arose

What a breathtaking sight my blessed eyes did behold
A splendid start of a story that just began to unfold

An enchanting mystery that only God could create
The strength of the connection I resolve to call fate

Some believe assuredly in love at first sight
Meeting you today I know they're positively right

BODY LANGUAGE

Our eyes met from a distance across the way
Not a word spoken, just a glance told all we wanted to say

A slight raise of the brow said you're interested in me
Much more to discover, to this we both would agree

The expression on our faces reveal what we now know inside
Something between us has happened which cannot be denied

The language of the body speaks more than words sometimes can
Let's take the time to explore what has already began

BY CANDLELIGHT

The room was lit by dancing candlelight
Seeing your beautiful face was my delight

Having pleasant conversation, I like your style
The sweetness of your voice and your girlish smile

Your eyes, so radiant, were a wonder to behold
Reflections I saw clearly like a window to your soul

Your skin all aglow as it was bathed in the light
Perfect were the moments and everything was right

Soft was the music, the right mood was set
The splendor of the evening, I will not soon forget

CAPTIVATED HEART

Never will I forget
When into my life you came
Call it love at first sight
Now nothing's the same

From morning to evening
And all thru the night
I stand amazed
You're such a lovely sight

Remembering the first touch
And the kiss you gave
Overwhelming love I received
And into my heart it was saved

Becoming one with you
As daily our lives blend
Discovering wondrous things about you
Like a story without end

CHANCE ENCOUNTER

I awoke this morning to thoughts about you
Beholding your face, wondering what to me you do

Remembering the whisper of your voice like the sweetest love song
Being sung to me now at the breaking of a new dawn

Should a chance encounter have such a lingering effect?
Wondering what things to come, what more to expect

These thoughts about you awakened me from a dream
The reality of you, so very splendid, a wondrous sight to be seen

Should a chance encounter have this lingering effect?
Wondering what things to come, what more to expect?

DATE OF FATE

What started as a casual blind date
Has become a moment of fate

When I met you on that night
Love began at first sight
We talked as friends from long ago
Sharing stories others didn't know

I felt I could tell you all
But decided to save some for when you called
What an evening and all it meant
Deciding you were heaven sent

Every story we exchanged
Made my life feel divinely arranged
Allowing me to meet just you
That one heart to hold forever true

What started as a casual blind date
Has become a moment of fate

DIAMOND

Today I found a treasure more precious than rare gold
Such intrinsic value, so very wondrous to behold

Stricken by your beauty, to which none other can compare
A radiant sparkling diamond, oh so very rare

To search the world all over, from the earth to the skies
No greater wonder can be found than when I look into your eyes

A vision of loveliness shaped by our Creator's hand
Endowed with grace and charm, the fairest in the land

Today I found a treasure more precious than rare gold
Such intrinsic value, so very wondrous to behold

DISTANT TOUCH

You touched me from a distance across the way
Not a word spoken, but I hear everything you say

Just to look into your eyes, knowing the treasure I've found
I hear music from heaven whenever you're around

The sun shines brighter with your every smile
The moon and the stars illuminate as they visit you for a while

The birds of nature gather to sing you a song
The wind gently whispers asking can it sing along

Everything about you changes life so much
Daily I yearn for your intimate distant touch

FIRST CONTACT

Late one night seen only by the moon's eyes
We sat under the stars and told of our lives
Understanding better why we are as we are
Sharing about the joys and pains we've endured thus far

Feeling free, but really being taken captive by thee
Knowing you, knowing me to a deeper degree
I reached to touch your hand as we begin to part
But I was really seeking to touch your heart

I softly caressed your face and ran my fingers through your hair
Hoping to convey my growing concern and utmost care
Feeling more comfortable, on me you gently leaned
Ever closer we drew, aware of what the moment would bring

A sweet gentle kiss, expressing more than words told
A second kiss more tender, imprinting my soul
The innocence of what we shared I shall not forget
Thoughts of our precious moments make my heart content

HIDDEN TREASURE

I've discovered a treasure
Of more value than the world's greatest pleasure

One that's unique and profound
Brings me much joy to be around

One that I long to have and hold
The anticipation of your love enraptures my soul

HIGHLIGHT OF THE SHOW

Not many days ago I attended a fashion show
Wasn't quite sure why I even decided to go
There was music, lights, and a touch of elegant style
Glitz and glamour as models strutted on stage and down isles

Each with beauty and splendor; so very much appeal
Until the highlight of the evening was finally revealed
For in walked you with a very regal stroll
Captivating my attention, a lovely wonder to behold

Such poise and charm, how could I not stare?
Gazing upon you, yet wondering if you were aware
My eyes fixed on you until the end of the event
Thinking how can I meet you and express my heart's intent

As the show ended and people browsed around
I drifted your way and this is what I found
Nice conversation, I really like your smile
I became very intrigued, as we talked a short while

I asked for your number when I had to go
You were the main attraction of the evening and highlight of the show

MORE TO COME...

I have thoughts about you throughout the day
Unspoken expressions of things I long to say

Words can't express the beauty of thee
Nor the awe in my heart at the splendor I see

As I gaze into your gorgeous eyes and behold your lovely face
I'm enchanted by an image that cannot be erased

Tender sweet lips I desire to softly kiss
Drawn by a passion I could never ever resist

You complete my world, making all things a delight
Now I understand the meaning of love at first sight

From the moment we met a mystery began to unfold
It will only be complete when it's you I finally hold

From the depths of my heart to the endless boundaries of my soul
There are deeper feelings for you that are yet to be told

MYSTERY

You're a mystery
That's intriguing me

I wonder what you hide
So way deep down inside

You look with piercing eyes
So simple, yet so wise

You slyly call my name
Tell me this is not a game

I'm constantly watching you
Liking what to me you do

You're a mystery
That's intriguing me

PERSONAL SPACE

You came into my personal space, but really I let you in
Coming over to talk was a nice way to begin

Usually I'm hesitant and it takes a while to drop my guard
But I felt secure with you and decided not to make conversation hard

We talked long hours about this and that
Your appealing eyes and pleasant smile, these I can't soon forget

The things said convinced me, with you I'd have no regret
I believe you understand as I do, we were destined to have met

I'm feeling close to you now, knowing we'll be more than just friends
You came into my personal space, but really I let you in

PRETTY PRINCESS

I met a pretty princess with fairytale charm
With a dancing smile and alluring eyes that bring no harm

Unaware of her own beauty, that could not be concealed
Lovely as a rose in bloom; a splendor ever being revealed

She has a rare name that is truly unique
A tender sweet heart that loves so deep

A priceless royal treasure that one should seek to find
All she has to offer is most truly divine

This elegant royal princess with a charming mystique
Gives such a tender love that it makes my world complete

RESPONDING TO YOU

From the very first moment we met
I knew my life would not be the same
You are the answer to all my heart's questions

As we talked I told you my secret dreams
Taking you to every place I've ever been
Sharing with you only all that's uniquely me

Exposing depths of my soul, yet feeling unashamed
Finding all I ever longed and searched for
Allows me to respond just to you

RIGHT PLACE AT THE RIGHT TIME

I had so much going on, I got there late
Should have been there at 7, but I arrived at 8

The crowd was loud, many people in the room
I decided to hang around to hear my favorite tune

I mingled around just to chit-chat
Before coming into the room where you sat

Our eyes met from across the way
At that moment I decided to stay

I casually walked over to politely speak
But found the one to make my life complete

Good conversation, I like the things you say
Having a good time as we talk and play

This fairytale story with a delightful end
Makes me think about how it all began

I had so much going on, I got there late
But really the time I arrived was an act of fate

SO SHY

You're so shy
I wonder why

With a lovely name
I will bring you no pain

Such a beautiful smile
Can we talk for a while?

Captivating are your eyes
Truthful, no lies

You're so shy
I wonder why

THAT NIGHT

On a boring Saturday night a few weeks ago
I visited a place that rarely I go

As I walked in, yours is the first face I see
Like an enchanted vision from heaven sent directly to me

Strikingly beautiful from head to toe
Capturing my attention, deeper than you know

Dance with me was my request of thee
You flashed a smile letting me know what could be

We held a brief conversation as we danced
This was a moment of fate and not by chance

Looking intensely into your eyes and searching to know
How deep into your world would you allow me to go?

As the night ended and we had to part
We walked out together and shared our hearts

I learned more about you as we stood and talked
Exchanging treasures that could not be bought

We made promises to see each other again soon
That we may finish the words of this romantic tune

WANTING TO KNOW YOU MORE

Just a brief introduction and you told me your name
Wanting to know you more is what my heart proclaims

Do you like long walks, I'm curious to know?
Or a favorite special place that you and I may go?

Asking others all around, "who's this woman of mystery?"
Beauty like none other that's captivating me

Elegant royal princess, certainly my first guess
Wanting to know you more, now my lifelong quest

WATCHING YOU

I've been watching you from afar
There's a radiance about you like a heavenly star
With pleasing looks, charm, and appeal
Thinking this is a dream, but praying that it's real

You smiled and walked toward my direction
About you I still had so many questions
As we talked we both had a similar reaction
Between us there was a mutual attraction

Discovering that while watching you, something I did not see
You only walked over because you had been constantly watching me

WHATEVER IT TAKES

What would it take to enter into your world?
Diamonds, rare jewels, or maybe precious pearls

Perhaps a noble task just to prove my worth
For you I would travel to the ends of the earth

Need I give you wealth or forsake my claim to fame?
All I would lay aside if your heart I would gain

Please tell me the secret that allows me close to your side
I promise an abiding love that could never be denied

WHEN I SAW YOU…

I walked into the room and saw you sitting there
Someone so very lovely, to look upon, I almost didn't dare

Breathtakingly beautiful, an angelic vision so rare
Stealing glimpses of you and wondering if you were aware

Such exquisite features, a princess with a royal air
Gorgeous lips and eyes, also the elegant style of your hair

I felt lost in a dream, but then I found you there
I'm enjoying this pleasant reality at which I intensely stare

Never wanting to forget the moment I saw you sitting there
Etched in my mind is a vision to which none will ever compare

SECTION II
True Soul Mate

Throughout life there are many opportunities to meet others and establish relationships. The difference about the soul mate relationship is how you seem to touch each other on a higher plain and deeper level. It bypasses the senses and reaches to an inner dimension only both your hearts know. Sometimes the knowledge of whom you've just encountered is instantaneous. At other times the reality of the experience is so deep it takes years to grasp that you're with the mate of your soul. No matter the time frame the result is always the same. Your soul mate is a combination of friend, lover, confidant, companion, teacher, student, your strength, your weakness, your true love, your greatest joy, and at times the cause of your deepest pain. No matter the role you will always know them as the mate of your soul.

ALONE TOGETHER IN A CROWD

Many people were in that same room
But only to your heartbeat was I in tune

So much noise others had to shout
All I heard was your sweet whisper round about

Even when the lights dimmed soft and low
Your face and eyes shone with a lovely glow

When we separated briefly to talk with friends
It was as countless moments I thought would never end

It's amazing how much I miss you so soon
Thoughts of your touch, lips, and scent of your sweet perfume

Although surrounded by many in a place that's loud
We're always alone together in a crowd

COMPLEXITY

Me you love, love you me
Oh what strange complexity

A random encounter, true love our hearts did find
By chance, not so, but by our Creator's design
First a vision of love we saw, has become a reality we now see
What was two, now becoming one, this truly meant to be

Seeking to know your thoughts and understand your mind
Still much unknown, but the answer is time
Through isolated feelings comes loneliness unaware
But holding and touching reassures innermost care

When unintentional hurt comes, from true love it will steal
Until we realize by love's strength, all hurt can be healed
Today becomes yesterday, tomorrow becomes today
All really we have is what our hearts let stay

Two lives starting a fresh, a fresh and a new
A never-ending start between I and you
Me you love, love you me
Oh what strange complexity

It's no secret love is the key
All in all
Simplicity

EXPERIENCE REAL LOVE

I see the depths of your heart, those things that make you cry
Yearning to experience real love, once hurt, yet willingly you try

I hear your prayers at night as you speak to heaven above
Asking when will that day come when you will experience real love?

Sometimes you look at others, to see how they relate
Wondering when to you will come, one to call soul mate

To give your heart to another, one that will be ever true
That blessed one will truly find heaven's reward is you

So much you want to give, so many just want to take
Finally one has come, to whose heart you can relate

Allow me to gently kiss away the depths of your hurt and pain
To touch and heal your heart that only real love may remain

FALLING IN LOVE

Falling in love was easy, upon those moments I now reflect
Playful days and comfortable nights, we experienced no regret

Each moment spent together seemed to never have an end
Never wanting to be apart from my close and intimate friend

Talking long hours as day blended into dark night
Losing ourselves in moments as we bonded close and tight

You became my only world around which my life revolved
Partaking of no single thing unless you were there involved

Nothing I'd not do for you, how strongly we'd relate
Denying others of my time, I've found one to call soul mate

Falling in love was easy, but truly I did not fall
Slowly love caressed my heart, and to you I gave my all

I'LL GO FIRST

Proceeding with caution and the utmost care
The delicacy of a once hurt heart, of this we're both aware

Now strongly drawn closer to each other
With feelings never having felt for another

Wanting to make my heart known to you, I'll go first
Unquenchable love I'm feeling, like a never-ending thirst

Wanting to share my lifelong dreams with only you
Together for endless days and long lasting nights too

I'm freely saying all these things, all so truly real
Love once kept hidden, now finally being revealed

I'll go first, knowing what I feel is right
Doing whatever it takes to make you the love of my life

IN THE MOMENT TOGETHER

We both see the same things
And we understand what they mean

What was said in the multitude of words
It feels good to know you hear what I heard

No lyrics, just soft music was played
But to us it was a beautiful love serenade

We're always in the moment together it seems
Our hearts are so close we have the same dreams

KISS AWAY THE TEARS

Whether it was thoughtless behavior or bad intent
Another brought you pain, no matter how it was meant

I look through the beauty and see the hurt in your eyes
From which teardrops have fallen as rain from cloudy skies

But now I've come to kiss away the tears
Removing the doubt and displacing the fears

He that treated you bad and the scars that were made
Allow me to give you the love that will make them all fade

For a heart held captive by hurt, I pay the ransom of love
As one that was sent directly from heaven above

For I have come to kiss away your tears
Removing the doubt and displacing all fears

KNOWING ME

I love it when you look at me
As your eyes explore my soul
You see me as I truly am and there's acceptance
All my aspirations, dreams, hopes, and very best intentions
Also my flaws, faults, fears, and insecurities
Yet your love surrounds and holds me
Making me stronger in every way

LET ME COUNT THE WAYS

Honesty…
Openness…
Communication…
Thoughtfulness…
Forgiveness…
Understanding…
Encouragement…
Support…
Concern…
Appreciation…
Gratitude…
Attentiveness…
Respect…
Commitment…
Loyalty…
Touching…
Holding…
Caressing…
Lovemaking…

NAKED

Only you can touch my heart and my treasured soul
Also my sacred body, to lovingly caress and hold

Giving all of me to you, so freely and unrestrained
Fully exposed to your eyes, yet feeling unashamed

Holding onto no secrets, letting you deep inside me
Knowing and exploring inner places none other will ever see

OVERWHELMING LOVE

I have a love that's overwhelming
Transcending endless time and the vastness of space
Surrounding you as air, so that you breathe me with every breath
So very close to you, I become your second skin
Wanting to dwell in your thoughts
That you may feel my very presence wherever you are
And hear my voice always in the depths of your soul

SOUL MATE I (I WANT TO KNOW YOU)

Give me the opportunity to earn your trust
By allowing me to appreciate all that's uniquely you

Tell me your most sincere hopes
And the strength of our love will bring them to pass

Show me your most precious dreams
And I promise together we'll make them a reality

Let me know what gives your heart the greatest pleasure
And I'll commit to never intentionally causing you pain

Share with me only your tender sweet love
And I'll always love you, adore you, and treat you as supreme

SOUL MATE II

You see what I say by understanding what I know
I say what you see by knowing what you understand

We can only be together if we're together when apart
Your strength my weakness, your weakness my strength

We're alone when not together, yet always together alone
I hear you although words are not spoken

I feel you without the slightest touch
Before we met I knew you, there was no need to be introduced

Now in love, we give love, to keep love, to have love, to make love,
    because we're in love

SOUL MATE III (FINDING YOU)

Alone no more
Since finding one I adore

Gone are the days
Of my mind being in a haze

I find security in your smile
As we talk for long whiles

Exposing depths of my soul
Things to others never told

Having feelings real and true
Deepening as I respond to you

Each touch is as a brand
Marking me as no other can

To only you I'm giving all
You're the answer to my heart's call

SOUL MATE IV (CHRISTIAN)

Our spirits are of like kind
Indwelt by the presence of our Lord

Our minds are totally on one accord
Not necessarily same thoughts, but same aim, purpose and intent

Our bodies walk in complete harmony
Because the path we take is to obtain the same goal

TRUE SOUL MATE

Laying here in the darkness of night, I hear you silently calling unto
  me
It's a captivating song played from dust til dawn quietly setting me free

Strongly drawn just to you when I see invisible things you do
You touch me oh so deep and all the love you give I keep

I can sense your presence so clear, even when not close, around or near
Your sweet echoing voice is heard without a single spoken word

You're in my heart and mind, and what we have is simply divine
Some have searched their whole life long to hear this unheard love
  song

What I've found in you I hold, the very special mate of my soul
And as our lives together unfold, a never-ending story is told
Of one more precious than gold, called the very mate of my soul

UNIQUELY YOU

The particular things about you, your uniqueness do they make
Shows you're extra special, your place none could ever take

Your walk, your talk, your smile, all beautiful and distinct
Whether near or far away, thoughts of you I think

So pleasing to the eye, even gorgeous to behold
Sharing with you an amazing love; blessed, I'm constantly told

I could never ask for more, to have someone love me so true
Many gifts sent from heaven, to me was sent uniquely you

X FACTOR

I've traveled the world to distant places
And seen the beauty of so many faces
Enjoyed fine dining with good atmosphere
Talked with lovely faces that drew near

Heard beautiful music as it was played
Often used it as a love serenade
Yet never finding a love that remained
That one same heart to forever claim

Then came you, heaven sent I'm sure
Making all worthwhile that I did endure
We talk long hours into the night
Thinking, "what about this one seems oh so right?"

Time we're together seems to multiply
It becomes unending, but I'm not sure why
Starting to wonder because of the care
And the thoughts of my heart you seem to place there

When apart from you it feels very strange
Like our being together should never change
Resigning finally, I can't figure it out
Many mysteries of God surround us all about

Us being together and how we connect
I've resolved to call it just factor X

ZONING TOGETHER

I love the place that you and I go
None can enter, only we know

Our thoughts become one, a single heartbeat heard
Even in silence there are spoken words

I look in your eyes and hear all you say
Telling me to forever remain this way

I think the thoughts that I hear you speak
Giving what you ask or need before you seek

I like the harmony that you and I share
Sometimes a different route taken, but still I find you there

Even when apart we keep the link
It's nice to feel the thoughts you think

It's very interesting that you know my mood
Happy or sad I always feel soothed

The connection shared is like a musical tone
Often called an intimate love zone

SECTION III
How We Relate

The way you relate to your soul mate is sometimes a mystery. You hear words that are not spoken and see that which is not revealed. There is between the both of you a knowing and relating that others cannot share in. But the knowledge of what it takes to keep this relationship in its unique harmony has to be tenderly cultivated. Be continually transparent, communicative, attentive, supportive, loving and nurturing. Always appreciate this special someone by saying and showing them how very much they mean to you. Find ways to express to this special person that they are an integral part of your life and are of extreme value and worth. For in loving and appreciating them you are loving and appreciating yourself, for they are the very best part of you. Celebrate them for who they are and not what they can do for you.

5 SENSES

Your **touch** awakens sensations locked deep inside
Only you possess the key to things I sought long to hide

The **taste** of your lips like fresh nectar sweet
More and more I'm enjoying this delightful treat

Your **eyes** pierce my spirit lovingly through and through
My inner most thoughts are never hidden from you

Your **fragrance** when close is so exhilarating
A high I yearn for so deliriously intoxicating

I can **hear** your heart beating a romantic symphony
Helplessly and willingly I draw closer to thee

APART TOGETHER

When we're apart to do our own thing
We're still together, here's what I mean

When out with the girls to share a laugh
Thoughts of me, through your mind pass
If a guy passed by dressed and well groomed
You think of the love we'll share soon

When the boys and me need our space
I see subtle reminders of your lovely face
A pretty face, body shapely and perfumed
Makes me think of secrets shared in our bedroom

When away at work to earn our pay
Still remembered are the sweet words we say
No matter the distance that separates us
We have a bond, a commitment and unshakeable trust

Having our space allows us to see
Apart together we'll always be

CHEMISTRY

We're attracted to each other, but I'm not sure why
A mixing and stirring when I look into your eye
Taken captive by your eyes as you slyly wink
Getting lost in the thoughts that you make me think

That certain subtle smile that makes me melt
Or the whisper of your voice that's deeply heard and felt
When you walk close by I feel arousing heat
Or a chill down the spine from my head to my feet

Alone or in a crowd I love to feel you near
As we whisper love secrets softly in the ear
Embracing ever tighter as we sensually kiss
Causing rapture to my soul as I experience this

Every touch on the skin causes passions to burn
The magic that we share can't be taught or learned
What we have together is often called a mystery
But the thing that we share is sweet chemistry

CONSIDERING US

Actions are louder than words, as the saying goes
One would be the wiser listening to someone who knows
The words "I love you" are very easy to say
But the real intent is in the price you're willing to pay

If my love is real it's freely given without knowingly hurting you
Considering what's best for our lives in all we say and do
Giving up the right if it ever becomes the wrong
Making all decisions to keep us ever strong

But it takes two, seeking to mutually agree and trust
Not choosing what's best for I and me, now ever considering us

COUNTING THE HOURS

I long to see you at 7, but the clock just now says 12
Thoughts of being with you is where my mind dwells

Another hour passed it's only now 1
Moments spent away from you seem like eons

Time is moving slowly the chimes ring at 2
Love touches my heart at every remembrance of you

A little bit closer, but still only 3
A special bond we share, oh how blessed is me

The waiting now half over at the stroke of 4
Soon I'll gaze into the eyes of the one I adore

Only two hours more the clock now says 5
We grow closer together each time we share our lives

Another glance at the clock it's right at 6
I now understand a love addiction, but in you I've found my fix

The moment finally comes as the clock now strikes 7
Each enchanted moment with you is like the splendor of heaven

EVERYTHING ABOUT YOU

I love the way you brush your hair
Of your every style, I'm always much aware

Those very pretty eyes into which I stare
The taste of your lips with every kiss we share

To feel your arms around me lets me know you care
No place I'll ever go without wanting you there

So great a love between us almost seems unfair
To be far away from you, this I'll never dare

Loving everything about you my special jewel so rare
So much we're together, moments away I can hardly bear

EVOLVE WITH ME

Our life together is a constant evolution
Let's make each experience a positive change,
That will serve to draw us ever closer

When things are good and everything is understood
Let's enjoy our smooth ride of laughter
When there's a bump in the road, let's still hold
And use it to connect ever tighter

When disappointment comes, let the direction you run
Be the one that leads directly to me
When one has success, let's be at our best
And realize we're a part of each other

When tempted to detour and things seem unsure
Let's talk and remember our commitment to this journey

As we were from the start, with love in our hearts
Through this evolution of change, let's ensure we remain
As we journey to higher plains of love

FOUND TRUE WEALTH

I saw two stars fall from the night skies
I found them in the radiant twinkle of your eyes

Reported lost was a priceless precious pearl
The value found in you is worth the wealth of the world

Gold was missing from a very secure domain
The heart of gold found in you is of the purest strain

Lost was a very rare jewel of riches untold
Still it in no way compares to what I feel when we hold

GORGEOUS EYES

I love your gorgeous eyes
They draw me deep inside
Revealing only unto me
Mysteries others cannot see

They speak silent words
So loud they can be heard
You're captivating me
Yet I feel so free

Piercing through my soul
Exploring things untold
Binding our hearts together
Outlasting always and forever

I love your gorgeous eyes
They draw me deep inside

GROWING TOGETHER

The person you are today
Is not who you will always be
The person I am today
Is not who I will always be

We shall grow in knowledge
We shall learn from experience
We shall be changed by each unique interaction with people and the
    world around us

Let's commit to always sharing our lives,
Sharing our experiences, and sharing our love for one another

With each passing day we shall become more attached,
More absorbed, interwoven, intertwined, entangled, blended,
Stirred, mixed, bonded and melted into each other
For in doing so, we shall never grow apart

HEART TALK

I love it when we talk
The sharing of our thoughts

To know you're listening to me
Always wanting things to this way be

For our future we make plans
Wondrous love between a woman and a man

Sometimes saying things more than twice
To understand each other is worth any price

Explaining in detail, sometimes we have to do
Helps you to know me and I to know you

I NEED YOU

Success on my own would not mean much
Empty and hollow, very cold to the touch

It's you I need and your loving embrace
Being held in your arms, a very comfortable place

Of the ones I've known, none a perfect fit
With you by my side, the loneliness I soon forget

No more could I ask for, all in you found indeed
Many things I have, but it's you I truly need

I WANT TO SHARE ME WITH YOU

For so very long I've kept myself distant from you
Not really knowing why, it was just the thing to do

But with you I'm starting to feel safe and secure
Beginning to even believe what we have can endure

There's really more to me than what meets the naked eye
In order to receive it, your love and trust I'll require

Respect and appreciate, this you must also do
Allows me to always say I want to share me with you

ARE YOU MAN ENOUGH?

This strong sensitive woman seeks your trust
Also inwardly wondering, "are you man enough?"

Sometimes this strong woman has been known to cry
Hoping you'll ask the questions to discover why

At times a little pushy, but this is only to make you aware
So much I have to offer, always show how deep you care

With just a little patience and also treat me kind
Then I'll show you a treasure others could never find

I have a deep love to give, this I truly do protect
No games or false claims, also promise me never to neglect

Just these things I ask and give me quality time
This wondrous love I'll share with you will simply be divine

I'M MAN ENOUGH

Dedicated to the end, even when the going is tough
Yes to the question, "am I man enough?"

Willing to commit real love, nothing fraud or fake
Strong sensitive woman I can heal your heartache

Not ashamed to share my feelings, the mark of a real man
Promising love in word and deed as no other can

Secure in my manhood, giving you freedom and your space
To be all you can be, takes us both to a higher place

Love, honor, and cherish, these things I'll also do
Letting none come between us, always caring just for you

Never seeing you as weak, just the tenderness of strong
Together with you in relationship that continues on and on

IN SICKNESS AND IN HEALTH

When there was sickness I knew all was well
You close by my side, my hand tightly held

Not at my best, moving at a slower pace
You to my rescue, to shield me from the race

When feeling down and needing a comforting word
Your daily "I love yous" are all I heard

Your care and concern brings me health
What I have in you is called priceless wealth

Quieted now was the gnawing and lingering fear
If not at my best would you still be here?

Deep down inside I know this to be true
When not at my best I can depend on you

LET'S NOT FORGET

From the start
I told you the secrets of my heart
I played no games
And made no false claims

I made a commitment to you
And spoke things that were true
To you only I gave my all
Because you heard the urgency of my heart's call

We seemed to always be in tune
Even when not in the same room
We talked about life's events
And always shared our true intents

We developed so much trust
Always having conversations about us
Knowing that we alone held the key
To ensure we would always be

Keeping what we have is my plea
The splendor of I and thee

LOVE IN ACTION

Love is more than just a spoken word
It's truly defined in the actions you observe

Don't be fooled by sweet somethings whispered in the ear
It's how you're treated when no one else is near

Love won't purposely hurt, forever it will abide
It seeks the best for you, pushing selfishness aside

Showing you its heart, so you'll know it's faithful and true
Trust me it asks, but first displaying it trusts you

Always building up and giving inner strength
Abuse, pain, neglect is never its intent

It speaks kind things when you're feeling down
Even when not at your best it stays around

It gives security by communicating, so there'll be no guessing
Sharing its hopes and dreams, it's such a wondrous blessing

It speaks the truth always for your greater good
To make you better as no other would

It will make a sacrifice in order to help you
All these things real love in action will do

LOVER & FRIEND

Deep satisfying relationship, you're my lover and friend
Sharing closeness and intimacy, our unique special blend

Late night talks while in bed we lie
Holding and caressing, nightly we try

When conflict comes I realize the enemy's not you
Resolving the problem together, this we both do

Committed to each other with steady unshakeable trust
Saying daily "I love yous" are a necessary must

When we're not together, memories still carried within
Always together in heart because we're both lover and friend

NOT THINKING OF YOU

Today I said I would not think of you
Then the sun rose in your form

I was concerned with other issues of life
But the clouds revealed your face

My mind was occupied with important thoughts and matters
It was the wind that whispered your name

As the cares of the day faded to night
The moon said you gave it the radiant light

I kept my word and didn't think of you today
But the stars sparkled like your eyes

NOTHING IS WRONG

I just want to let you know nothing is wrong
More good days than bad days as we sail along

To talk things over is such a nice treat
It helps secure the love we promised to keep

The thoughtful things you do make my heart soar
I thought it not possible, but daily I love you more

Again I say to you nothing is wrong
Our days and nights are still as a romantic song

PRECIOUS JEWEL

You're my unique rare jewel

Sparkling eyes

Radiant smile

Ruby lips

Heart of gold

Diamond love

Precious as pearl

QUIET TIMES

During those quiet times I can still hear your love
It comes floating to me on the wings of a dove

On a bright peaceful day or the silence of a dark night
Your love rides on the wind, seen yet hidden from sight

That certain way you look with unspoken words all about
I feel your love surrounding me like an unending echoing shout

You say so many meaningful things with a sweet gentle touch
And the long lingering passionate kiss tells me ever so much

During those quiet times I can still hear your love
It comes floating to me on the wings of a dove

THE REAL YOU

This beauty I see that stands before me
From where did you truly come?

Please tell me the story of your radiant glory
The life experiences that have brought you to me

So when I see a smile on your face I'll understand its place
That I may deeply share your laughter

Or the tear in your eye if ever I see you cry
So I may bring comfort that really matters

To know the things that you fear when doubt comes near
That you may know you can trust me

To know the real you and all you've been through
Allows me to love you even stronger

THE WAYS OF LOVE

Just calling to say hey
Several times a day
Letting you know
How much I love you so

Thinking about you
And the sweet things you do
Passing the time with haste
Until I see your lovely face

Let's spend time alone
While I sing you love songs
About special things we share
For you I'll always care

TO HOLD ME

"When can I hold you?" is what I heard you say
By willing to truly know me is the only way

Listen to my thoughts and you'll understand my mind
Hear just not my words, it's my heart you must find

Appreciate my unique life and the struggles I've been through
What I have to offer is most precious, real and true

Also I must trust you, so please don't treat me wrong
Always know the deeper meaning of my favorite love song

Only then can you hold me, because I'll feel you now know
What it takes to keep me and to none other would I go

TO RAISE A CHILD

It's an awesome responsibility to raise a child
Not a short-term commitment, it lasts for a while

It's both our duty, each doing our part
An extension of our love, to which we give our heart

We train by example about the ways of life
Discussing what's best as we guard against strife

Teaching this child the way to go
Defining "yes" and explaining the reason for "no"

We pull together using the best from our past
Making joint decisions to raise a child of class

We teach morals and values that will make strong
And how to make choices between right and wrong

As this child grows, maturing more each day
We'll stay involved, helping define the way

Giving love and guidance to fill the heart
Praying that from the right path in life, they shall never part

VISIONS

Unforgettable, that's what you are, as the song goes
I find traces of everything we shared, like petals of a scattered rose

Glimpses of you are seen in the early hours of the morn
I reach for you, but embrace only the shadow of a distant form

In every ray of sunshine at the breaking of a beautiful dawn
I see the bright color of your eyes in the rising eastern sun

Every breath of the wind brings your fragrance fresh and clear
Also it sweetly whispers your name, bringing you ever so near

The reflection of your face is seen in windows along the street
Hoping it's you, I quickly turn, it's like a splendid game of hide and
    seek

Throughout the day I'm constantly seeing beautiful visions that seem
    true
None are as lovely as the one I gaze upon when I'm finally back with
    you

WHEN YOU NEED YOUR SPACE

I saw you cry and I'm not sure why
Please tell me if something is wrong
Explain to me the tear as I draw you near
Trust me to hold you and make you strong

Was it something you heard or an unkind word?
Together we'll try to make things better
I'll kiss the frown from your face and put joy in its place
My love is here even in bad weather

Talking to me allows us to be
Always share what is the matter
What causes you fear, I'll always be here
Let's bond and grow in love together

Don't pull away cause you think I won't stay
There are many unknowns in silence
If you need your space, which may be the case
Then let this be your reliance

You have a choice speaks my comforting voice
The commitment we have is true
No matter what you choose, you will not lose
I'm patiently waiting to love you

YET I BEHELD YOUR FACE...

A solar eclipse darkened the skies, yet I beheld your lovely face
The luminous moon lit up the night, yet I beheld your lovely face
Stars of heaven shown so bright, yet I beheld your lovely face
Streaking comets appeared in space, yet I beheld your lovely face
These heavenly wonders are marvelous sights, yet I behold your lovely
    face

SECTION IV
Love Vows

When the time comes for "I Do" commit to never letting it become undone. The richness of the eternal union between a man and a woman should be a celebration of joy. This unending journey should be entered into with the deepest of thought, reflection, fear and courage, and also with a knowing that the love within each of you is enough to overcome every obstacle and challenge that would seek to break the bond. Remember true love never fails and is everlasting.

AS ONE

It feels like a dream
That's how it seems
What does it really mean?
Two hearts and lives joined as one
Sharing in love, caring in love, loving in love

How it all began…
With a subtle glance
Noticing you from afar
But of this you were unaware
Thinking, such an elegant lady as me
Of beauty, charm, grace, and appeal
A truly unique design
When will all this his blind eyes see?

I'm a deep distant brother, not like every other
A caring intense lover
Was it a chance encounter or a moment meant to be?
They call it destiny
I'll make the first move, for her I'll drop my cool
At last my queen sent from God
Knowing now, we truly belong

Single steady raindrops become a flood
A raging storm was once a gentle breeze
The passion for you, once an ember
The love for you, now a blazing flame

Arriving at this special day
Before our Creator and all to say

I will, I do, never ever to be undone
Two hearts and lives joined as one

FROM TWO TO ONE

From two to one, a divine mystery
Stronger now together, than one could ever be

Like pieces of a puzzle make a picture complete
Only one with the other can greater heights be reached

By respecting differences deeper depths are known
Walking a path together that one could not walk alone

Not always seeing eye to eye, sometimes differing points of view
But willing to work it out is the best that we can do

The key to remaining together when being pulled apart
Is remembering our commitment and the love shared at the start

LOVE VOWS

This woman only will I have and hold
Loving her always from the depths of my soul

Cherishing my queen, this I'll sincerely do
Staying always faithful and forever true

Honoring her as beautiful, intelligent, and wise
Thanking God daily for such a heavenly prize

Through sickness and health my love will not fail
The power of love is eternal and shall always prevail

Rich or poor, through these I'll also stay
Asking God's blessing is what I'll constantly pray

Today before all let this story be told
This woman only will I have and hold
Loving her always from the depths of my soul

UNENDING LOVE

Until the sun no longer shines
And the oceans are dry as desert sand
When all the stars can be counted
Or the stormy wind be contained
If every mountain was made a hill
And the earth no longer turned
Yet my love for you would never end

WITH THIS RING I THEE WED

You're the one who makes my heart complete
Two once alone, now becoming one unique

A bond, a closeness, a forever connection
A knowing touch, a tender kiss, mutually shared affection

Mystery of mysteries divinely planned
Eternal union remembered with a touch of your hand

Holding you close until one heartbeat is heard
Hearing "I love you" in every spoken word

Every thought now considering you
A resounding echo of an unending I do

I now we, from mine to ours, me becomes us
Wonder of wonders as we love and trust

With this ring I thee wed
Worn as a token of all the love we pledge

YOU

Exquisite creation from above to make my world complete
To awaken and behold you, fashioned so rare and so unique

Not the awesome sky above, nor any wonder in the whole land
Compare to the pleasures felt from a single touch of your hand

The most precious diamond in the earth and the brightest star in vast
   space
Bow to your radiant beauty and the lovely splendor of your face

In those very pretty eyes I see how marvelous heaven is to be
Always am I blessed when those eyes look at me

I promise to love thee both now and forever more
Now life holds new meaning since I'm with the one I adore

YOU'RE MY TRANSCENDENT LOVE

In the deepest recesses of my mind there stands an image of you
It takes shape and forms the epitome of everything a woman should be

The inner beauty of your pure love flows out creating a river of life
Bringing harmony to everything it touches, bringing joy to the deepest
pain

Your every expression carries with it the force to change the world
around you
Nothing that comes into your presence leaves the same; an evolution
from good to better

Your radiant beauty transcends the physical and even touches on a
higher plain
Eyes that sparkle, lips soft as clouds, hair silky smooth, a fragrance like
the morning rain

When we caress and hold every touch intensely ignites the flame of the
soul
Sweeping us away to distant places that usher us deeper into this
rapture of love

SECTION V
Working It Out (In)

Be very aware there will come disagreement, argument, misunderstanding, frustration, and for periods of time, unexplainable distance. Just know assuredly these things only arise to allow you to go to deeper levels of intimacy and connectedness. Talk it over, shout it out, cry together, and show that you are willing to fight for the uniqueness of your love. The fight is not with each other, but with the situation, the circumstance, or the thing that is issuing a challenge to say "you won't last". At those times fight to reconnect, not to stay disconnected. Remember how things were at the beginning. It wasn't about I, you, me, yours or mine. It was all about us. Always seek that which will be the best for "us". Forgive, forget, be considerate, and be fair and truthful in your dealings with each other. If you practice these relational truths things can and will come back together, only stronger and better.

A SINGLE TEARDROP

The single teardrop that gently fell
Served to let me know all was not well

I had promised neither to hurt nor to make you cry
But this single teardrop I cannot deny

The disappointing things both done and said
Seek now to destroy all the happiness ahead

From this moment on I will bring pain no more
Especially to the one whom I truly adore

To wash away the hurt and restore the beauty of it all
Was because of a single teardrop that did gently fall

ACCOUNTABILITY

Accountability is not control
We're just sharing those things that should be told
Working together and being at ease
Feels so good, just like a summer breeze

All big decisions, let's please discuss
Helping to ensure there will always be an "us"
This doesn't mean, you I don't trust
Being in agreement is a necessary must

Please don't assume about something I do
Just ask why, and I will explain it to you
Sharing with each other our points of view
Allows us to hear and know what's true

Speak your mind and feel free to share
Being concerned let's me know you care
Accountability is not control
It shows commitment to each other as our lives unfold

AFTER THE ARGUMENT

What happened to the love we promised to share?
Committing to each other to always be there

Hurtful words spoken without thought or care
Both of us heartbroken and full of despair

Now returning to our senses and being made aware
Neither right, nor wrong; both being very unfair

If our love is real, unique and rare
Being apart, we could never stand to bear

Whatever the damage, we'll both seek to repair
Destroying what we have, we should never ever dare

ANOTHER CHANCE

Please give me another chance
I promise to give sweet romance
Your birthday, I won't neglect
Nor will I give your heart more regret

The hurtful things I will not choose
Nor your love will I abuse

The little things I failed to do
I want to make it up to you

Some things you've heard all before
But this cry please don't ignore

No longer will I cause you pain
Because of some childish or silly game

So very much, you mean to me
Apart from you I cannot be

Please give me another chance
I promise to give sweet romance
Your birthday, I won't neglect
Nor will I give your heart more regret

AT OUR BEST

As you can see we sometimes disagree
It's called exploring all our options

To be at our best for each challenge and test
Let's talk and share our laughter

To say "I'm wrong" is not a sad song
It helps us find the right answer

When "I'm sorry" is due after discovering the true
To say so makes us stronger

When I feel weak and it's you I seek
I draw strength from your embrace

If together we'll be, just I and thee
Let's open up and share our hearts

BUSINESS MANAGEMENT/ RELATIONSHIP MANAGEMENT 101

In corporate America we have a meeting each day
To discuss our plans that will guide our way

To accomplish our vision and reach each goal
We discuss what to do and define each role

We formulate strategy for the company's success
Discussing openly what practice is best

Every idea we cannot always use
Only those that support corporate views

When problems arise that can hamper success
We don't blame the person we blame the process

We have meetings and share data to determine root cause
Agreeing to make changes when we identify flaws

When financial challenges come to cause delay
We reprioritize the budget to clear the way

Open communication helps us flow with change
Understanding the reasons when plans are rearranged

Longevity, profitability and a good reputable name
Is how we measure performance to ensure our fame

So much to do to make the company a success
Each doing their all and being at their best

CAN WE MAKE IT NOW?

When the weather was fair and we didn't have a care
It was easy to share our love

When the days were sunny and bees brought their honey
Our words were soft and sweet

When life gave no test and we were at our best
We playfully skipped along

There was music each day and an abundance of pay
We heard every bird sing a song

Now dark clouds have rolled in and a cold bitter wind
A challenge they have to offer

The days are long and there's no fairy tale song
The music has been turned to silence

Now can we make it and calmly take it?
The punches of life have been thrown

Now we'll represent our heart's true intent
Tears are now our laughter

Can we make it now…?

COME WHAT MAY

Through thick and thin my love will abide
Reserved just for you, never to be denied

Staying together not always easy, tough some would say
I for you, you for me, come whatever may

Sometimes mistakes are made that will drive us apart
Distance comes to show what's really inside the heart

Even a silly break-up does not have to be an end
If love was real in both our hearts, somehow we'll start again

DEEP LOVE

Real love when truly given is never hard
Constantly doing things to draw together, not apart

Although hurt and sometimes misused in times past
Still it seeks commitment that will ultimately last

Ever striving to connect with a kindred soul
To give itself completely, reaching for depths untold

The voice of deep love not all can hear
Its cry is only understood by a heart that's shed a love tear

DISTANCE HAS COME

I thought I was close to the one who mattered most
The one called my true love

How could I not see the insecurity in thee
And speak comforting words of love

Although in the same place, being together may not be the case
If there is distance deep in the heart

It may have come to do us great harm
But let's use it as a way to better show
That distance came to allow our love deeper places to grow

FAR AWAY NEAR MY HEART

Transcending the distance, yearnings now consume my heart
Thoughts become feelings, stronger now we're apart

Fleeting images, really visions of you
Occupying my days, and night dreams, there too

Wanting to hold and commune with thee
Sharing precious moments of things yet to be

Longings of the soul, for you running deep
Promises spoken, these yet we shall keep

Far away near my heart I feel
Distance comes only to establish what's real

FORCES OF NATURE

Even in the mist of a **thunderstorm**
My unending love for you goes on and on

Thunder & lightening, rain & hail
Being together forever, these things can't prevail

Then came a fierce **hurricane**
It passed over and our love remained

A sudden **blizzard** with knee-deep snow
Melted by the passion of the love we show

A **heat wave** came with raging fire and flame
Our intense love made that appear as an ember; small and tame

Tornadoes swept across the land
The strength of our love endured again

A **volcano** erupted with lava all ablaze
It went unnoticed, only at your loveliness do I gaze

An **earthquake** ripped and tore apart the land
But even more powerful is the love I feel with a touch of your hand

Also the destructive fury of a **tidal wave**
Can never wash away the memories of all the love we gave

I NEED TIME

I'm mad at you because of what was done and said
It's hard to see the happiness ahead

Don't come near me or I might shout
I need some time to sort things out

To be sincerely honest and speak the true
Things like this push me away from you

The one you hurt is the one you love
These words apply to you, my love

What was your thought or your intent?
To me explain, how this was meant

We are so close, yet this still came
But I know in time, it won't remain

Not telling you of the lingering effect
Would someday cause deep regret

Even through this I still love you
Just please learn of what not to do

Surely I forgive and also forget
I just need time to think through it

IF IT MATTERS SAY SO

At times I'm not sure what has brought you pain
Never intending to hurt, it's your love I seek to gain

If it ever really matters, please always tell me so
Those things important to you, I'm willing to know

Pride never the issue, nor the silly game of shame
How could I go through life, if together we not remain?

So if ever feeling less than my lovely noble queen
Remind me of this promise to treat you as supreme

INNER FEAR

I sense in your heart an inner fear
Threatening the closeness we both hold dear

From whence it came, past hurts I'm sure
Don't treat me as the problem, my love is pure

Always by your side, my commitment please trust
Willing to resolve issues, so there'll always be an us

Let's talk about the hurt hidden deeply inside
It we have to conquer for our love to abide

JUST LIKE THAT...

Words were spoken that I'm not sure about
Still circling in my mind like a distant shout

I'm a bit quiet now just trying to think clear
Trying to discover what has brought us here

Out of frustration something had to be said
But let this not spoil all the happiness ahead

The sad look in your eye, you feel the same as I do
Even this matter we still will come through

After further reflection I think I now know
Why this direction our hearts must now go

If we are to draw closer then this is the test
A journey taking us from better to best

As we talk things over being very sincere
Understanding comes as we tenderly hear

Through this conversation I now certainly detect
Our heart's utmost desire is to reconnect

I feel love washing away what sought to hold us back
Our bond has grown stronger just like that...

LET'S RESOLVE THE ISSUES

I'm not the domineering person you could not please
Nor the uninvolved one that abandoned you with ease

I'm not that first love that made you cry
Who gave no reasons when you asked "why?"

I'm not the one who didn't communicate
Because of them you find it hard to relate

I'm aware of those times that you push me away
Because of the others who would not stay

I can see your doubt when the going gets tough
Silently asking, "will there always be an us?"

I understand your need to be in control
Because of hurt done by others, who promised to hold

I hear in your voice a defensive attitude
Protecting a tender heart, that's often been used

To make a mistake doesn't make you bad
Nor should others who envy you make you feel sad

When you become quiet I sense the scare
Placed there by others who really didn't care

So much beauty, yet you seem to choose
To allow others to take advantage and use

I'm here to love you and be involved
Facing the issues to be resolved

MAKE THIS WRONG RIGHT

Every morning that I wake up
All I think about is our recent break-up

My heart is filled with sadness from sun up to sun down
It's just not the same not having you around

My days are empty and I'm sleepless every night
All my thoughts are of you and of how to make this wrong right

Us getting back together shows broken hearts can mend
From now til always and ever, let's not let this happen again

Real love has a way of overcoming every trial and difficult test
But making up makes it all worthwhile, only then do we see love at its
   best

POINTLESS MATTER

It doesn't really matter who was right or who was wrong
How sad we no longer hear the words to our song

Music we once danced to with unheard beat
This others around us still wonder and seek

Our hearts now distant over a pointless matter
Lifelong dreams would we so easily shatter

Let's talk things over voicing our concerns
Needing you close again, for this my heart yearns

I'm sorry for what happened, let's lay it all aside
You and I forever together is how we should always abide

Let's come back together

POWER STRUGGLE

What are these struggles for power we seem to display?
We disregard each other just to get our own way

A constant debate that neither of us can win
The way we treat each other can be described as sin

Is it so important just to prove a point?
A battle neither of us wins, it's like a limb out of joint

To be together this must be resolved
I believe in us, let's remain deeply involved

Both committing to change and to began to really live
Being no longer selfish, we'll mutually give

Please trust my heart, you I will not lose
Nor your love will I ever abuse

To struggle for power is a really bad choice
Let's remain strong as a single voice

All our shared dreams can come to past
Working together to ensure we last

Being honest and open, let's not pretend
We'll make mutual decisions so we both win

READ BETWEEN THE LINES

Our recent time together held no special meaning

It was refreshing to have conversation of such caring

We had nothing in common except being in the same place

I was lost in the moment, but aware of a bond developing between us

I wasn't paying attention, not really hearing what you said

Daily I find my mind filled with memories and thoughts of you

There's no need to see each other again, nothing could ever be

Do call or come over, I'm longing to hear from you again

Read between the lines

REAL LOVE RISING

Sometimes things don't go as we dream
Life's disappointments aren't always as they seem

We're not together now, our world has been torn apart
But now a deeper love is rising in the heart

Eyes now being opened with renewed sight
Seeing each other now in a different light

Better than before, now lovers and friends
Restoring of hopes and freely giving love again

No one could have known a break-up would be a start
Of a deeper, purer love rising in the heart

REMEMBER THE GOOD TIMES

Sadly gone are the days when everything between us was fine
Never a hurting word spoken, always trying to be kind

There was love and laughter, the negatives we chose not to see
They were not important if our love was to continue to be

Let's remember the good times, forgetting them we never should
I think we'll discover it was our love that made the times good

So let's rekindle love's passion no matter the cost
Talking, touching, holding, all these we should have never lost

Let's remember the good times, forgetting them we never should
I think we'll discover it was our love that made the times good

RUNNING AWAY TO YOU

You tell me things I don't want to hear
Things I ponder when you're not near

You say you love me, but I push you away
Keep listening closer, I'm really saying stay

You ask to come over and I tell you no
But my heart wants you here and to never let you go

The gifts you give are no special treat
I throw none away, all of them I keep

I try hard to deny what to me you do
Over and over I find myself running away to you

SEE EYE TO EYE

Allows a deeper love when seeing eye to eye
To know and understand, always we must try

Sometimes what I mean is not always as I say
Silly little things called words get in the way

Also are the things that never I should have done
Forgive and forget, for me you're the only one

Trying to straighten it out sometimes makes it worse
Forever please remember what we had from the first

SOMETHING HAS TO CHANGE

You walked away from me in cold silence
Our being able to talk had always been my one reliance

I reach for you now and emptiness fills my grasp
Me only trying to hold us together is too awesome of a task

What happened to bring us to this terrible lonely place?
Daily I search my mind for ways to bring a smile to your face

The abiding love I feel for you will always remain
We can't continue as we are something has to change

Look deep in your heart to find the love we once shared
There's too much between us for which we both once cared

STAYING IN LOVE

I remember the words I often heard, "unto you I give my all"
After many years of some pain and tears, I realize there's been a fall

Oh how we started so great, me and my precious soul mate
Now painfully clear distance is here, hardly ever do we relate

I ask the question, "how do we stay in love when being pulled apart?"
Daily no fresh deposits of love are being stored deep within my heart

I look at the events, from where were they sent, to draw away my true
love?
When they came like a wicked game, I should have looked to heaven
above

The answer has come to recover us from harm, restoring all that was
lost
Asking forgiveness from you of the things I do, too great has been the
cost

As we tenderly hear and speak things sincere, distance cannot reside
Making the necessary change that we remain, our love to ever abide

Staying in love takes effort and thought, ever considering us
Drawing close to talk it out, is an absolute necessary must

Learning daily and watching out for things against me and thee
Sharing a strong and solid trust allows us to always be

STRENGTHEN OUR BOND

About the heated talk we had just last night
We tossed and turned without sleep; let's make it right

Please know that I'm sorry, this was not my intent
Even the choice of words is not what I meant

Didn't mean to disappoint, and yes I do care
Differing expectations, we both must be aware

I cannot read your mind, your thoughts I have to hear
Explaining the reason makes things crystal clear

Sometimes we're as one, same thoughts do we think
These are just growing moments when we seem out of sync

This I believe and assuredly know
When we strengthen our bond conflict has to go

THE CALL

I was so glad you answered
When I ventured to call
What seemed to be risky
Was not a risk at all

I've had time to think about
The things of which I'm now ashamed
I'm willing to change whatever
To ensure our love remains

Let me make it all up to you
For I'm the one to blame
Me who once caused hurt
Will now bring joy, not pain

THE CURE

It's late at night and I'm pacing the floor
Driven by something I can no longer ignore

I've finally come to realize
I'm only content when gazing into your eyes

I'm hard to deal with, so I've been told
The only comfort I find is when we hold

Eat or sleep, both hard to do
Nothing is right when apart from you

Fever, aches and all sorts of pain
A kiss from you and it can't remain

Dr's orders and of this I'm sure
Getting back together with you is my only cure

THE ORIGIN OF PEARLS

When wounded by you, I tirelessly search for the real intent
Discovering that into my openness you've come, no matter how it was
    meant

The thing that caused the hurt and the depth of pain
Strangely I embrace it, although not wanting it to remain

As you cover me with your love and enter deeper into my world
The hurt begins to change to become the most beautiful pearl

THE TEST OF REAL LOVE

What were we thinking when we decided to part?
We had a very strong bond, we shared the same heart
Distance came, we let other meaningless things in
That, learned from mistakes should not be repeated again

How can this blaze of love that once wildly flamed,
Have now diminished and be filled with such pain?
Through this masquerade we try to go on with life
Our once peaceful garden now has thorns and strife

We called each other soul mate and promised to forever hold
Now what we have to offer is very sad and cold
If our love is true it will pass this test
At the worst in life love will show its best

I still believe in us even through this pain
In the heat of the desert an intense thirst is gained
We now thirst to love with an unquenchable desire
But now it's purer, it's been tried by fire

This was a good place where we have been
It has strengthened our love that we may start again
Now we've learned, discovering what this all meant
A love mate of the soul is truly heaven sent

THE TRUTH AND THE LIE

The truth is that I hurt you
The lie is that is what I intended to do

The truth is I will make effort not to let it happen again
The lie is not to trust me or to listen to bad advice from a friend

The truth is you know my love is real
The lie is to think me hurting you was no big deal

The truth is I miss you and you're my life's delight
The lie would be to continue on and not make this wrong right

THOUGHTS OF YOU

Late at night sitting alone in the dark
My mind was filled with thoughts of you
That certain way you smile and laugh
Those lovely eyes and your sweet fragrance when near
Your gentle and tender touch
All the things you do to show you care
It's said that absence makes the heart grow fonder
I find this to be so very true
It's late at night and I'm having thoughts of you

TRUE INTIMACY

The physical act is most certainly good
Being intimate together, we often should
But there are other things we have to relate
And for granted, we must not take

Are we treated well when no other is near?
When bad weather comes will we still be here?
Are your ways meant to drive me away?
How often heard are words that say stay?

Are intimate secrets shared just between us?
When times are hard do we still have trust?
Can we talk together about the rain?
Or certain things that cause us pain?

The questions I have, we have to know
To bring us closer, so love can grow
What would you do to prove to me,
Us being together is important to thee?

The physical act is most certainly good
True intimacy comes from being understood

WHAT'S REALLY IMPORTANT?

Certain things in life, so callous and cold
Only warmth I find is when we hold

Some problems and issues are an everyday thing
We'll handle them together or distance they'll bring

What's really important is the uniqueness of us
Establishing a life built on love and trust

Always we understand, together are you and me
As we deal with challenges and work hard to agree

WORKING IT OUT

This is going to be tough, but it has to be said
I'm not sensing the love that we both once pledged
We sometimes talk, but don't communicate
There's not much meaning in the things we relate

Our listening skills are lacking at best
Still this is a necessary and passable test
We must identify the reasons we fight
Both points of view are probably right

None of this means I don't love you
Remember our promise to speak the true
This is a dark and very wicked game
We have to conquer it, so we may remain

Hear my story and point of view
To understand what I'm going through
Talk to me and plead your case
So the distance that's come can be erased

We will last and get past this
Our solemn duty, we won't be remiss
No abuse, not a scream, nor an irrational shout
Let's intensely talk together and work it out

WRONG DECISION

I made a wrong decision
Now things are in derision

Next time I'll think twice
And positively ask for your advice

At first I didn't want you to know
Because I feared the words "I told you so"

I'm glad nothing critical comes from thee
Stronger your love flows to me

For in this time of my regret
You chose to forgive and to forget

A sincere apology from my heart
Allows us to began a fresh new start

SECTION VI
Romance

Always remember the flame of romance should never be extinguished. Romantic intimacy is a life force that sustains and maintains the passion of the relationship. Take the time and make the effort to keep spice in your love life. Romance doesn't always have to be a big major event, but it should be a life-style of doing little, continual, and sweet memorable things that can only be shared between the two of you. The reward you stand to gain from what you invest in the romance will be well worth any effort. Touch, kiss, embrace, hold, and caress. Do nice pleasing "just for you" type treats for one another. True love can never hold its distance from the object of its desire, nor will it fail to show "you are special to me" in its actions.

A COLD WINTER'S NIGHT

On a cold winter's night not so very long ago
Relaxing by the fireplace flame, our faces all aglow

Classical jazz heard in the background nice and low
Cuddling close, kissing and touching, soft and oh so slow

Words of love whispered only you and I will ever know
Taking us to our special place where none but us can go

Both secretly wishing this night would never end, although
Knowing we'll begin again with a stronger love to show

A KISS

Revealed through a kiss
All I ever missed

Taking my breath away
Now my life's in disarray

Awaking calling your name
Feelings so strong I feel ashamed

Wanting to be with you
Do you feel the same way too?

Revealed through a kiss
All I ever missed

A RAINY NIGHT

Steady falling raindrops lit by the moon's light
Low rumbling thunder and lightning all through the night
Lying together with candles burning, but not too bright
Gazing into your eyes and thinking what a lovely sight
Sharing a love that's real and we both feel it's truly right
Stronger the love grows as the rain pours on a dark and rainy night

ANTHEM OF LOVE

Vision of loveliness, this ascribed to you
Real life splendid dream, said about you too

If I had just one wish, I'd wish with all my might
To be in your presence morning, noon, and thru the night

Enjoying your conversation, shared with me alone
Exchanging our life stories like sweet romantic songs

I love to softly whisper nice somethings in your ear
Also very pleasing is your fragrance when I draw you near

Holding each other kissing slow and long
You and I together, precious love forever strong

BODY MASSAGE

A body massage from head to feet,
With kisses and bites is very sweet

Every caress causes a rush
A tingle is felt with every touch

A sensual sigh when the right spot is found
A meaningful moan is a pleasurable sound

Nice hot oils rubbed with care
Scented candles that fill the air

Romantic music that fills the room
And the soothing sound of a favorite love tune

A body massage from head to toe
Creating memories that only we know

DESSERT

A full course meal is very filling indeed
Satisfying the appetite is a basic human need

Delectable dishes, to the pallet they do appeal
Tasteful delights that appear almost unreal

After finishing a well-prepared meal I always have dessert

Savoring every bite of this delightful treat
Succulent pleasure that tastes so sweet

Taking my time as I delicately bite
The more I partake increases my appetite

You are my dessert

EVERYDAY LOVE

Songs of love, precious gifts or roses to you I give
You're the love of my life, I'm so very fulfilled

All these are just a token of what is real
True expressions of love ever being revealed

Today and everyday surrendering all of me to you
Always keeping love secrets of the special things we do

FOREPLAY

I give you attention and quality time
Listening to your thoughts and the ideas of your mind

When you ask of me, something to do for you
It becomes all-important, because it's important to you

If a choice has to be made about what is priority one
Let there be no worry, you are second to none

What we have is rare and a delightful mix
Even spending time at an occasional chick flick

Then...

When I kiss your lips and draw you tenderly near
There's no remembrance of times you needed me and I wasn't here

When I kiss you on the neck and caress your face
You have no thoughts about being second place

When there's a sensual desire and a passionate embrace
Not knowing your concerns, will never be the case

When I touch your body for pleasurable desire
Never will you say, "he doesn't know me, nor the things I require"

When making love to you there will never be a day
That your thoughts are, "he doesn't listen to a word I say"

FOREVER NEAR

I never really knew love until I met you
Thoughts of closeness and sharing in all we do

Stealing away to secret places, you and I alone
Scented candles and music that played our favorite song

Sharing a love that's oh so right, going on and on
Drawing closer together to stay forever strong

Can't make it through the day, unless your voice I hear
Those sweet things you say, in my heart I hold dear

Never letting you far, when at arms length, I draw you near
Always kissing and holding to stay forever near

FULFILLED

My heart deeply overflows
When with you, out comes poetry and prose

Singing to you songs of love
Because you came directly from heaven above

Giving you sweet romantic things
The kind of things only found in dreams

Sitting with you under the stars at night
As we make plans for our future, feeling oh so right

Thinking how much I like having you around
A wondrous treasure only I have found

Forever giving you a love that's true
Daily finding ways to keep passion fresh and new

HEAD TO TOE

The penetrating gaze of your **<u>eyes</u>** is what drew me
I seemed to be hypnotized, even mesmerized

Tender sweet **<u>lips</u>** I love to kiss
Each kiss is as a gift in which I find passion and pleasure

The strength of your **<u>embrace</u>** draws and holds me near
So ever close that I find myself lost in you

The ground you **<u>walk</u>** on, to me is blessed earth
Even nature responds as a rose blooms in your every footstep

HOT TUB OR JACUZZI

I remember the water had a sensual flow
It took us to places that only we know

The swirling current with relaxing heat
Was very stimulating from head to feet

Also the kisses were wet and sweet
Leaving memories of a pleasurable treat

I remember the water had a sensual flow
It took us to places that only we know

I WATCH YOU SLEEP

Often late at night I watch you sleep
Wondering what memories in the heart you keep

Sometimes you utter faint words I barely hear
Then I whisper softly "I love you too my dear"

A kiss on your cheeks, then your lips I do taste
Lovingly I brush back your hair and a smile comes to your face

As if sensing my presence you draw close to caress
Still soundly sleeping you lay your head gently on my chest

Often late at night I watch you sleep
Wondering what memories in the heart you keep

IN SYNC

Moving in rhythm
As passions flow

Even breathing as one
Deep and slow

Even our hearts
Are on the same beat

Two as one
How very unique

INTIMACY

I love touching your hair
And caressing your face
Kissing your neck
Then your lips I taste

Holding you close
In a loving embrace
Feeling the warmth of your body
What a comfortable place

Wondering how close
We can really be
Enjoying the depth of love
That flows from you to me

INTIMATE DISTANCE

When away from you I still feel intimacy
Even when distant I'm connected to thee

Someone at work wore your favorite perfume
All I could think about was our candlelit bedroom

Your picture I keep so nicely framed
Causes passionate stirrings, both wild and tame

When words are spoken that remind me of you
I have vivid memories of the sweet things we do

Every time I hear your voice on the phone
I anticipate the moments when we're together alone

As the radio played our favorite love song
I could still feel the kisses shared; intense and strong

As I walked outside and felt the summer breeze
I thought of the many ways you so deeply please

Several times a day I softly whisper your name
Thinking about the love secrets that yet remain

When away from you I still feel intimacy
Even when distant I'm connected to thee

KISSABLE LIPS

You have kissable lips that I love to taste
A sensual mouth and a very lovely face

I love to kiss you slow and long
Or with passion, intense and strong

With each kiss comes a pleasurable surprise
Like rays of sunshine from beautiful skies

Sometime the kisses bring a meaningful moan
Like the first note of our favorite love song

Or there are times a sensual sigh is heard
That could not be explained by the spoken word

Soft sweet lips that take my breath away
Getting lost in the moments as night turns to day

You have kissable lips that I love to taste
A sensual mouth and a very lovely face

LET ME IMPRESS YOU

Let me impress you and occupy your time
Alone, a quiet evening to wine and dine

Roses I give you to set the right mood
Anxious anticipation, just being with you soothed

Afterwards we talk with low lights and soft jazz
Appreciating you with sweet somethings worthy of a woman of your
    class

Or maybe we could walk hand in hand by the sea
Our footprints in the sand for time and eternity

I would give you the moon and the heavenly stars
Saturn, Jupiter, Neptune, also Venus and Mars

Let me impress you and occupy your time

LIKE A ROSE

Beautiful and delicate like a splendid rose
Alluring the heart to reach out to touch
But carefully handling this enchanting loveliness
For this we truly know, a rose has thorns
Not as a weapon to inflict pain
But only as a reminder to hold with delicate care
This you are so very wondrous to behold
Always to be treated like a splendid rose

LOVE GAMES

Let's go to the drive-inn and make out in the car
Or at night on a blanket making love under a star

A secret rendezvous, as we rent a private room
Filled with burning candles and sensual love tunes

Or leave a trail of notes guiding you far away
Meeting me at a place prepared for us to play

The sheerest lingerie from secrets Vickie shares
You and I enjoying pleasures, while hiding out from other cares

Or pretending to be a pirate enjoying spoils from a war
And you the lovely damsel taken captive from afar

Or take a trip to a land that's not so very near
Wine, fine dining and very romantic atmosphere

Or cruise to an island in the middle of the sea
Getting lost in passionate moments shared only by me and thee

Or just staying at home cuddling close in our room
Late at night, curtains open, making love under the moon

Ever playing games of love reserved just for us
Keeping spice in our love life is an absolute necessary must

LOVE IOU

There may be times we seem out of sync
When my thoughts for love are not the same as you think

If you're tired and run down and I'm in the mood
Just give a love IOU, so you don't appear rude

To plan our intimacy is not so strange
As we set aside time, so there'll be no change

Through the business of life, our love we will guard
Enjoying each other is the sweetest reward

LOVE IS LIKE SNOW

Just as every snowflake differs
No two loves are exactly alike
My love for you is not like any other

Snow falls light and gentle to the ground
But becomes heavier and deeper the more it falls
The love I feel for you grows heavier with each passing day
It gently rests in the depths of my heart

At night it's wondrous to behold snow covered sights
My love will cover you from harm, hurt and
All that would seek to divide us

Snow ultimately fades away, yet forever remains in a different form
My love for you may not always be flashy or showy, but
It will forever remain in the form of a passionate kiss,
A loving embrace, or a tender touch
Always letting you know love is like snow

LOVE LESSONS

Called Casanova, Don Juan or maybe Romeo
There are still many lessons of love that you need to know

Lovely Juliet, Queen Cleopatra, or the beautiful Helen of Troy
Still there's much to learn about love that will bring you joy

Like the meaning of a kiss and how deep it goes
Causing a rush to the head and a curl to the toes

Or a touch so hot it causes passionate flames
It starts a sigh, then a moan, as ongoing pleasure is gained

Then the kiss on the neck that takes the breath away
Leaving exhilaration that words cannot speak or say

An intense embrace from which the sun would melt
A deep penetrating love both heard and felt

To caress the body until the senses tingle with fire
Unleashing sensations that have an insatiable desire

Or to share a oneness, so there's no longer two
Making love together the whole night thru

The deep lessons of love are as a musical tone
Exquisite sweet sounds, passionate rhythms, and resounding
    harmonies we seek to make known

LOVER'S SLEEP

Closing our eyes enjoying what we yet feel
Some may call it fantasy, but we know it's truly real

Still speaking softly, so much we want to say
Describing every moment of why we feel this way

Remembering lasting touches shared by me and thee
Letting none come between us, this way we'll always be

Still feeling the love from our head to our feet
Holding each other close as we drift into lover's sleep

LOVING YOU: MIND & BODY

Mind
The deepest things about you I know
Those secrets to me you've only dared show

I understand the very thoughts of your mind
When with you there's no such thing as time

Your every action, no need to explain
The misunderstood, soon becomes plain

That certain look you give is no longer a mystery
Silent words spoken, just between me and thee

Body
The slightest touch becomes a flame
A slow burning fire when I hear your name

Every sweet kiss and tender caress
Starts good, gets better, then finally the best

Swept up in passion like a turbulent storm
Giving unending love that rages on and on

Loving you is both body & mind
Sharing a bond unbroken by the passage of time

MAGNIFICENT LOVE

I appreciate your love and your every tender touch
The deep care of your heart that gives so much

When I need to talk, you give comforting words
In the sweetest voice I've ever heard

Every sacrifice you make and the nice things you do
There's no greater love as magnificent as you

MEMORIES OF LOVE

I love to feel you in my arms
When I tenderly draw you close
Melting and blending together
As we embark on this passionate journey

I inhale the fragrance of your hair
The aroma of your perfume
And the sensual sweet incense of your body
As we begin to slowly simmer in the flames of love

Showering you with kisses
From your head to your feet
Touching you as an exquisite treasure
Both priceless and unique

Each kiss and touch is as a brand
That marks the very soul
Imprinting deep memories
That we shall forever hold

Love songs created by sounds, rhythms, and harmonies
That only you and I can sing
No one knows the words
That we have heard

But they will forever be shared
As love secrets between me and thee

MIDNIGHT SERENADE

A still moonlit night
Oh so soft and very bright

Dazzling bright stars fill the vast sky
Expressly for you and I

A single musical note
Becomes a meaningful love song

Always when we're together alone
At midnight

MY GIFT OF LOVE

Many expressions of love are offered this time of the year
Varieties of gifts given as tokens, though not always sincere

Unto you my most precious possession is given, it's called the purest
love
With you only, sharing this splendor sent on wings from heaven above

Promising never to be seasonal or occasional, only constant and clear
Otherwise how would you know you're special and oh so very dear

Encouraging your heart through life's thunderous and raging storms
Quietly whispering "this will pass", as love's strength endures on

Sometimes I appear tough, challenging, and calmly strong
This is only to merge closer as deeper levels of intimacy are born

To our bright future I gaze, but occasionally reminiscent of the past
Making our best better, and refining the possibilities to ensure we last

MY VALENTINE

A day represented by hearts
But the day will pass
The truth of our love
Is what ultimately lasts

We say things like "happy valentine"
And "would you be mine?"
But after all is said
It's what's done that really defines

My feelings are not limited
To one day of persuasion
This love for you will be displayed
At each and every occasion

Always my love

NEED I SAY MORE?

You and I…
Soft music…
Low lights…
Or candle light…
Sweet kisses…
Tender touches…
Loving embrace…
Through the night…
Into the day…
Need I say more?

OH HOW I LOVE THEE

For the sweetness of your love, oh how my heart does ache
A longing deep within my soul, for you alone I wait

The brightest day is dark as night without you by my side
Sun and moon see my tears, those which I cannot hide

The pleasure of your love, I feel, and never can I ignore
Caressing deeply heart and soul, this touch I do live for

To feel you in my arms again, makes my world revolve
To taste your lips and warm embrace, now all life's mysteries solved

The moments I make love to you, days and nights do blend
Eternally shall my love not stop; there shall never be an end

OUR SONG

Lives in harmony, a beautifully blended tune
Like notes of a melody from which a song blooms
Rhythms of love, music we only hear
A soft and sweet serenade as we draw near

PASSION

Longing for you with anticipation
Your closeness causes exhilaration

Awaiting your every tender kiss
Whenever away you're truly missed

Loving to softly caress your face
As we're alone together in a secluded place

Holding to each other making love
Under moonlit sky with stars above

PASSION'S EMBRACE

Each touch ignites a flame
A burning pleasure, both wild and tame

An intensely raging fire
With an all consuming desire

Heightened sensations almost extreme
Reality becomes like a dream

As we melt into passion's embrace
Losing track of time and place

PLAYFULNESS

Laughing and playing are very sweet sounds
Kissing and touching as we wrestle around

Holding you down and kissing your face
Sharing a love bite in a memorable place

A playful slap on the butt is fun
Or I chase you around when you try to run

Also the times we play hide and seek
With every find there's a special treat

Laughing and playing, and kidding around
Allows me to enjoy the treasure I've found

PLAYTIME (GAME #1)

On slips of paper we write our desire
Making known what we intimately require

The 3-minute rule is our guide
Once the request is made it cannot be denied

A toss of the coin decides the 1st to go
No one loses, this we both know

I like this game, but this is what I've found
We break the rules at the start of the second round

PUBLIC DISPLAY OF AFFECTION

I love our private times when passions flow
Heard, said and done are things that only you and I know

But I also like affections in public display
A statement of what we share while at home or away

I don't mind the touch that someone else may see
It let's me know you're connected to me

When we feel the urge to share a kiss
Being drawn to each other; just can't resist

Enjoying an embrace right in plain view
Liking everything about what to me you do

When I draw close to softly whisper in your ear
It's really no secret; I just like having you near

This is not a game or to put on a show
What we have together we already know

The beauty of what we share is very hard to conceal
So deeply we love, it's just publicly revealed

REKINDLE THE FIRE

Starting truly to miss those romantic times once shared
Songs and candlelight dining, expressing how we both cared

Stealing away for precious moments to places none other could go
Never doubtful of your love, because you always told me so

Memorable kisses and lasting embraces, I miss so very much
Also those pleasant times when we lived for each love touch

Passion seemed to last for endless days and long nights on end
Let's take time to recapture how things were when we first began

REMIND ME...

If I fail to say "I love you" each day
Tell me of my actions

If I give you no rose and don't acknowledge new clothes
Remind me of happily ever after

If we ever fail to kiss or an embrace is missed
Just place your hand gently in mine

If I don't draw you near and whisper in your ear
Then lay your head on my heart

If passion seems gone and I sing you no song
Just come and hold me tighter

Always remind me of the worth of thee
Because it's us that really matters

ROMANTIC EXPRESSIONS

Remember the rose petals scattered on the floor
Making a trail leading to the bedroom door

Or by the fireplace with a nice burning flame
Slowly making love, softly whispering your name

Following written notes that would lead to a surprise
Enjoying the pleasure of the look in your eyes

Also the arrangement of our secret rendezvous
Expressions of a heart that truly loves you

SANDY BEACH

Under the stars and by the moon's light
On a nice sandy beach, what a memorable night

With music and drinks, on a blanket we lay
Kissing and holding as we intimately play

The crash of the waves provided pleasant sound
As we explore pleasures being sweetly found

The roar of the ocean in the background low
Will keep the love secrets that only we know

Under the stars and by the moon's light
On a nice sandy beach, what a memorable night

SILKS, SATINS, AND LACE

Smooth silks
Shimmering satins
Tantalizing lace
Letting our imaginations run wild
The rest is up to us

SLOW BURNING CANDLE

I lit a candle to awaken the night
A very slow burning flame, but not too bright

Your piercing eyes that touch my soul
Awaken passions that can't be told

Drawn to you by this dancing flame
Sharing love none but us can claim

A caress so sweet that I can taste
A touch so deep we dare not haste

We make love intense and strong
As the candle burns the whole night long

SUNRISE

Each morning I wake up to a glorious sunrise
My day becomes brighter as the sun opens her eyes

Radiating beauty, a most precious fair sight
Displacing darkness and shadows with a radiant and bright light

I felt the warmth of the sun gently kiss my face
Stirring a shared passion that can not be erased

Each touch from the sun causes a sensual flame
Igniting levels of pleasure that will daily remain

I'm alive with life with the sun's every embrace
Our exquisite intense journey to a very memorable place

Engulfed by a light that penetrates the regions of my soul
My sweet morning sunrise, forever I'll tenderly hold

The love of my life I call my morning sunrise
A daily present to me, my beautiful heavenly prize

SUNSET

In the twilight of the evening my sun begins to set
Enchanting hues of color, with memories I'll never forget

Drawing me close as it melts into the evening sky
Awakening sensations that I could never deny

My caressing sunset with mysterious hues
Shares with me treasures that we mutually choose

No need for a candle to offer luminous light
The beauty of my sunset; a very splendid sight

Each moment we're together is like a dream without end
Transcending to distant places to daily draw close again

I call my love sunset because she colors my sky
With exotic arrays of passion as together we lie

THE MEANING OF TOUCH

With my eyes I behold you
A breathtaking beauty, I do see
Causing stirrings in my mind
Captivating thoughts about what could be

Wondering if this is a dream
From which I will soon awake
Or a heavenly vision
To which I only can relate

But only through touch do I truly understand
So many things explained when I gently touch your hand
A thousand words are spoken of how I'm truly missed
But only do I feel it all through a tender sweet kiss

Expressions of our love are whispered in the ear
But clearly is it understood when I caress and draw you near
Each time we make love together, I hear so much
A million things explained through the meaning of touch

THIEF

I've come to steal your heart away
With gifts of love and sweet things to say

I'll treat you like a fairytale queen
But this reality will be better than a dream

Poetry, soft music as we wine and dine
Low lights or candles expressly to make you mine

I have come to steal your heart away
With gifts of love and sweet things to say

TIMELESSNESS

When you and I are alone together
I wish each moment was a separate forever

Let time stop and remain absolutely still
As we explore deeply what our hearts strongly feel

Enjoying intimacy we need not rush
The universe itself has stopped with a hush

When you and I are alone together
I wish each moment was a separate forever

UNDIVIDED ATTENTION

You've been working very hard, so let's steal away
To a nice secluded place just to hide-away

Oh by the way, when we get there
Just one thing of which I want to make you aware

Your undivided attention is what I'll require
You meet others requests, now fulfill my desire

Really this is not a selfish thing
If we don't have our time, distance it will bring

Nothing is as important as the beauty of us
Having times of undivided attention is a necessary must

UNENDING AND COMPLETE

I have come to give you a love
That will sweep you off your feet
A love that's sweet and gentle
Yet unending and complete

One that satisfies the heart
And also caresses the soul
Ascending us to the heights of heaven
To explore mysteries untold

Deepening daily to regions yet unknown
A descent without end, made together not alone

I have come to give you a love
That will sweep you off your feet
A love that's sweet and gentle
Yet unending and complete

UTMOST

Unquenchable passion, none can tame
Insatiable desire, almost like pain

Intensely yearning for your touch
Your forever embrace, I want so much

Your continual caress, for this I live
Everlasting love, to you I give

WET KISSES

As we stand in the shower
In a passionate embrace
Sharing wet kisses
That I love to taste

Each caress ignites a burning flame
Even the water could never tame

As the water flows
From head to toe
It takes us to places
That only we know

Whenever it rains
From heaven above
I remember wet kisses
Shared with my love

WHENEVER...

Whenever I need to see you, I look in the heavenly skies
In the moon and the stars above me, I see the beauty of your eyes

Whenever I need to hear you, I ask angels to sing a song
By the sweetness of your voice, I find strength to carry on

Whenever I need to sense you, I ask the wind to blow my way
It brings to me your fragrance that lasts all through each day

But whenever I need to kiss you, it's your lips I must taste
Nothing can compare, nor your sweetness be replaced

And whenever I need to touch you, I stop time on earth and space
Intimately so close with you, enjoying passion's embrace

YOUR TOUCH...

Your touch...
Makes me burn
For you I yearn
Now no concern
Mutual love returned
Your touch...

Your touch...
You I can trust
I feel a rush
Makes me sigh
I wonder why
Your touch...

Your touch...
First I'm weak
Then I'm strong
I hear a song
Going on and on
Your touch...

Your touch...
Please come near
So you can hear
What I feel
This is real
Your touch...

SECTION VII
Happily Ever After

The love of your life, no matter how perfect they may appear to be, will have their share of faults and flaws. These are things you should not be critical of, but accepted as a quirky part of this wonderful person you love so dearly. Some habits they'll change, some they won't, but all in all you have to know what's really important. Focus on the positives rather than spending time on annoying negatives. The soul mate relationship is one that endures through the trials, tribulations, setbacks, disappointments, challenges, and triumphs of life. Enjoy the moments, don't sweat the small stuff, and keep a sense of humor in all things.

BEFORE & AFTER

There were breathtaking moments, as love swept us away
Now in a routine, it's just another ordinary day

Passion went for days and long nights on end
When are you coming home from hanging out with your friends?

There was so much conversation, so much to talk about
Now for your attention, I have to scream or shout

You would climb the highest mountain just to see me
Please stop channel surfing and watching satellite TV

Everything was romance and soft candlelight
Now you snore, pull the covers and stink the night

There was love in the mornings, passions filled our room
Do we have time for a quickie; the kids will be home soon

You loved to take me shopping; I dressed very sexy and sheer
I didn't sneak and buy this outfit; I've had it since last year (lie)

You dressed your best, had good manners, and wore nice cologne
Now I have to train you before you leave home

We've grown stronger in love, all can plainly see
Appreciating each other allows us to always be

ROMANCE AND REALITY

A lady of elegance; smooth skin and scented perfumes
Still, please close the door when you're in the bathroom

Such a handsome gentleman all polished and neat
Why are there still issues about the toilet seat?

When you approach me for passion with dashing wit and charm
A shave, a shower, and deodorant would do you no harm

You smother me with kisses til there's no relief
Please try a breath mint or just brush your teeth

There was once sexy undies and sheer lingerie
Stay out of those old t-shirts, nightly I pray

Memories of painted nails and well kept hair
I would gladly pay the price for your beauty care

There were muscles, bulging biceps, and washboard abs
As you hold me now it's love handles I grab

A once shapely body, well toned legs and a tight derriere
Exercise for you now means a run to the easy chair

Still we have love that was meant to last
Some things are unimportant that we can look past

THE JOYS OF LIFE

Every day was passion, we christened each room
Now we lock the doors, the kids will be home soon

Wine and fine dining, daily there was a rose
Very practical are we now, the kids need new clothes

Fairytale princess and prince charming dancing in the rain
Whose turn is it now to pick the kids up from the game?

Traveling to distant places, kissing under a full moon
Plumbing broke, flooded carpet; the repairman will be here soon

Each day there was a gift or a nice sweet surprise
Now we watch the budget, the company is talking downsize

There was music in the air and never a harsh word
Explain to me now what it is you think you just heard

Friends and family were pleasant and truly heaven sent
Now they get not one more dime or a single red cent

These are the joys of life, so much do we gain
Growing through each moment with stronger love as our claim

978-0-595-35865-6
0-595-35865-9